"I CAN'T TAKE YOU ANYWHERE!"

First Aladdin Paperbacks edition March 2001

Aladdin Paperbacks
An imprint of Simon & Schuster Children's Publishing Division
1230 Avenue of the Americas
New York, NY 10020

Also available in an Atheneum Books for Young Readers hardcover edition.

Designed by Nina Barnett.

The text for this book was set in 18-point Berkeley Book.

The illustrations were rendered in pen-and-ink and watercolor.

Printed and bound in the United States of America

2 4 6 8 10 9 7 5 3 1

The Library of Congress has cataloged the hardcover edition as follows:

Naylor, Phyllis Reynolds.
I can't take you anywhere / by Phyllis Reynolds Naylor ; illustrated by Jef Kaminsky.
p.   cm.
Summary: When the klutzy Amy Audrey Perkins is as good as gold at Aunt Linda's
wedding her relatives are so surprised that they have an accident.
ISBN: 0-689-31966-5 (hc.)
[1. Clumsiness—Fiction. 2. Aunts—Fiction. 3. Uncles—Fiction. 4. Weddings—Fiction.] I. Kaminsky, Jef, ill. II. Title.
PZ7.N24Iaac   1997
[E]—dc20   96-7768

ISBN: 0-689-84116-7 (Aladdin pbk.)

"I CAN'T TAKE YOU ANYWHERE!"

PHYLLIS REYNOLDS NAYLOR
illustrated by JEF KAMINSKY

Aladdin Paperbacks
New York London Toronto Sydney Singapore

To Stephanie Altemus, with love
—P. R. N.

For Mom, Dad, and Mia
— J. K.

Amy Audrey Perkins was sort of a klutz.

She spilled things.

She dropped things.

She stumbled.

She tripped.

She was never quite sure how it happened. One minute she would be calmly eating a strawberry cone, and the next, the ice cream would be in her lap.

Mr. and Mrs. Perkins knew quite well what to expect, and so they preferred not to take their daughter anywhere.

They worked from morning till evening, and on weekends they liked to stay home and eat toast.

Amy's mother and father swung her high in the swing and played Monopoly with her at the table. But if they went anywhere, they went alone.

Amy's grandmother took care of her each day after school.
She and Amy baked cookies.
They planted flowers in the garden.
They read books on the porch.
But for some reason, they didn't go anywhere either.

It was Amy's aunts and uncles who went places.

They went to museums.

They went to church.

They ate in fine restaurants and liked to shop.

"Take me with you!" Amy said to Uncle Fred.

So Uncle Fred took her to the museum.

Amy stopped at the fountain to watch the goldfish. She leaned too far over and fell halfway in.

"Amy Audrey, I declare! I can't take you anywhere!" said Uncle Fred, looking embarrassed.

And when he took her home, he said to her parents, "Never again!"

"Take me with you!" Amy said to Aunt Susan.

So Aunt Susan took her to church.

When the offering plate was passed around, Amy dropped it.

Dimes and quarters rolled across the floor. Amy had to crawl under the pews to pick them up.

"Amy Audrey, I declare! I can't take you anywhere!" whispered Aunt Susan. And when she brought her home again, she told Amy's mother, "Never again!"

"Take me with you!" Amy said to Uncle Charlie.

So Uncle Charlie took her to dinner at a restaurant.

Amy reached for the butter and knocked over her water glass. Water spilled all over the table and dribbled down into Uncle Charlie's lap.

"Amy Audrey, I declare! I can't take you anywhere!" Uncle Charlie scolded, wiping up the water. And when he brought her home, he said to her father, "Never again!"

"Take me shopping!" Amy said to Aunt Jean.

"Well, I don't know, Amy. I've been hearing things about you," Aunt Jean told her.

"I'll be good as gold," Amy promised.

So Aunt Jean took her shopping. But before she knew it, Amy was going up the escalator and Aunt Jean was going down.

And as soon as Amy got on the down escalator, she saw Aunt Jean going up.

"Amy Audrey, I declare! I can't take you anywhere!" Aunt Jean said when they finally found each other. And when she brought her home, Aunt Jean looked at Amy's mother and silently shook her head.

Amy was feeling sad. Aunt Linda was getting married, and Amy wasn't sure she was invited.

It would be a fancy wedding.

Everyone would have on their best clothes.

After the ceremony they would eat from fancy plates with fancy silverware.

Amy's parents and grandmother were going. All the grown-ups were going.

"Take me with you!" Amy begged her mother. "I want to go to the wedding more than I want skates.

"I want to go to the wedding more than I want a bike.

"I want to go to Aunt Linda's wedding more than I want a triple chocolate sundae with hot fudge sauce."

"Relax," said Mother. "We'll take you, but for heaven's sake, Amy Audrey, be careful! Don't be such a klutz."

The day of the wedding, Amy put on her best dress, her socks with the lace around the tops, and her pink shoes.

She sat very still in church. She didn't cough, sneeze, or burp.

She did not stumble, trip, or fall down the steps, and she stood quietly outside the church when the bride and groom came out.

At the wedding dinner with the fancy plates and silverware, Amy did not spill the water.

She did not drop her fork.

She took small bites of wedding cake and even remembered to chew with her mouth closed.

Aunt Susan was so surprised at how well Amy was doing that *she* dropped *her* fork.

Uncle Fred, who was passing by, reached down to pick it up.

Aunt Jean, who was walking behind Uncle Fred, bumped into him and sent him sprawling.

Uncle Charlie reached down to help up Uncle Fred, and tripped a
waiter who was carrying a tray high in the air.

The tray came down with a crash.

Salmon all over Aunt Susan.

Fruit on Uncle Fred.

Jelly on Aunt Jean's blue jacket.

And cheese on Uncle Charlie.

Amy Audrey Perkins quietly looked at the mess around her and said, "Aunts and Uncles, I declare! I can't take you anywhere!" and went on eating her cake.